RADICAL ACCEPTANCE

A 10-Week Journal for Taking Charge of Your Life

Dr. Don Schweitzer, PhD, LMSW

Radical Acceptance:
A 10-Week Journal for Taking Charge of Your Life

Editor: Paule Patterson

Artwork provided by: Vecteezy.com

Cover design: Paule Patterson

Published by: Sierra Counseling and Coaching

Publisher Website: https://www.sierracounselingandcoaching.com

The moral rights of the author have been asserted.

For permissions inquiries, please contact:
Dr. Don Schweitzer
P.O. Box 122
Forest Grove, OR 97116
don@sierracounselingandcoaching.com

TABLE OF CONTENTS

AN INTRODUCTION

Welcome to a personal journal on a transformative journey for Radical Acceptance. In this sacred space, you will embark on a profound exploration of embracing life as it is, freeing yourself from the shackles of resistance, and finding inner peace. Radical acceptance is an invitation to meet each moment with openness, compassion, and non-judgment. Through the pages of this journal, you will delve into the depths of self-discovery, uncovering the power of acceptance to heal, grow, and live authentically.

Radical acceptance is about acknowledging and embracing reality as it unfolds, even when it doesn't align with our desires or expectations. It is a courageous choice to relinquish control and surrender to the present moment, allowing life to be exactly as it is. Throughout this journal, you will be encouraged to explore the stories, beliefs, and attachments that prevent you from accepting what is. By cultivating awareness and compassion, you will discover the freedom that comes from letting go of resistance and embracing life's inherent uncertainties.

Within these pages, you will encounter thought-provoking prompts and reflections designed to guide you on your path of radical acceptance. You will have the opportunity to explore challenging situations, past regrets, and unmet expectations with kindness and understanding. Through this process, you will gain insights into the patterns of resistance that have kept you stuck and discover new pathways to emotional liberation.

Radical acceptance extends beyond accepting external circumstances; it encompasses embracing your true self; flaws and all. It does not mean passively accepting or condoning harmful behavior, but rather accepting the reality of the situation without fighting against it or trying to change it in that particular moment. Throughout this journal, you will be invited to explore your inner landscape with compassion and self-love. By confronting self-judgment and embracing your authentic essence, you will unlock the transformative power of radical self-acceptance, paving the way for personal growth and fulfillment.

Radical acceptance is a practice, not an endpoint. It requires patience, resilience, and a willingness to confront discomfort. This journal will serve as your companion, supporting you through the highs and lows of your exploration. Embrace the process and trust that each entry is an invitation for you to take another step closer to the profound peace and serenity that comes with radical acceptance.

Remember, this journal is your safe space to express yourself authentically, free from judgment or limitations. No one else is here to read what you write. Allow your pen to flow, uncovering the truths that reside within you. Embrace vulnerability and cultivate a loving curiosity as you delve into the depths of radical acceptance. May this journal be a catalyst for personal growth, self-compassion, and a profound shift in how you navigate the world. Prepare to embark on a journey that can forever transform your relationship with yourself

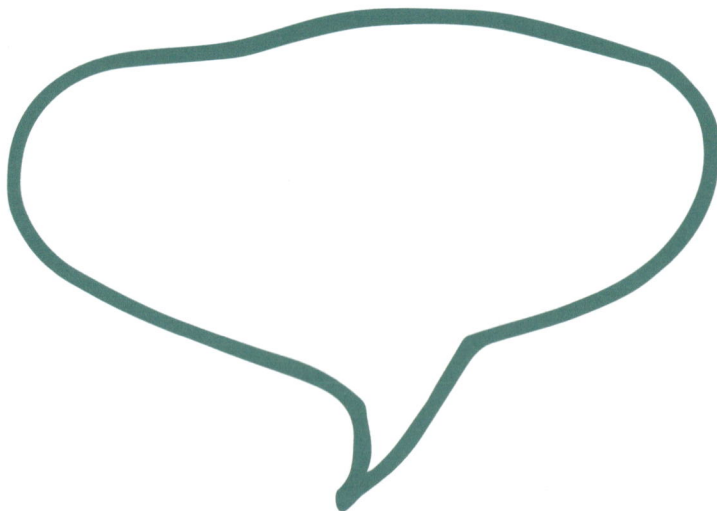

BENEFITS OF JOURNALING

Although this journal is focused on acceptance, the benefits of journaling on a wide range of thoughts, experiences, and reflections holds tremendous significance in our lives. It serves as a powerful tool for personal growth, self-discovery, and emotional well-being. The process of actually writing out our thoughts allows us to gain clarity, process complex emotions, and explore our innermost desires and aspirations. Here are several reasons why journaling is essential:

Firstly, journaling acts as a form of self-expression. It provides a safe space to articulate our thoughts and feelings without judgment. By writing freely and honestly, we can release pent-up emotions, frustrations, and anxieties, which can be incredibly cathartic. It helps us develop a deeper understanding of ourselves and our experiences, leading to increased self-awareness and personal insight. By practicing journaling, we practice being better at communicating with ourselves and others about ourselves.

Secondly, journaling promotes mindfulness and reflection. Taking the time to reflect on our day, our actions, and our goals allows us to pause and gain perspective. Through journaling, we can evaluate our choices, identify patterns, and make connections that we may have missed otherwise. It enables us to learn from our experiences, both positive and negative, and make more informed decisions in the future.

Thirdly, journaling serves as a means to record our memories. Our lives are filled with countless moments, big and small, that shape who we are. By documenting these moments, we create a tangible record of our journey through life. Years later, we can revisit these entries and relive cherished memories, gain fresh insights, and see how far we have come. Journaling becomes a precious gift to our future selves, a testament to our growth and resilience.

Fourthly, journaling is a valuable problem-solving tool. When faced with challenges or dilemmas, writing about them allows us to externalize our thoughts and gain a clearer perspective on our dilemmas. We can analyze situations objectively, brainstorm possible solutions, and weigh the pros and cons. The act of organizing our thoughts on paper often leads to new insights and creative ideas that may have remained hidden in the recesses of our minds.

Lastly, journaling promotes personal accountability and goal setting. By documenting our goals and aspirations, we create a sense of commitment to ourselves. We are able to confront in a safe space our own selves. Regularly writing about our progress and setbacks holds us accountable for taking action towards our dreams. It also allows us to track our growth, celebrate achievements, and adjust our strategies when needed.

Journaling is a powerful practice that benefits our mental, emotional, and even physical well-being. It offers a creative outlet for self-expression, fosters self-awareness and mindfulness, preserves our memories, helps us solve problems, and promotes personal accountability. Whether it's a daily ritual or an occasional practice, the act of journaling invites us to explore our inner landscape and make sense of the world around us. Any level of journaling is better than none. So, grab a pen and a notebook, or open a document on your computer, and begin the journey of self-discovery through the transformative power of journaling.

JOURNALING TIPS

Choose the right journal: Find a journal that you feel comfortable writing in. It can be a physical notebook, a digital document, or a dedicated journaling app or website.

Set aside time: Dedicate a specific time each day or week for journaling. It could be when you first get up, before bed, or during the day. Consistency is key, make it a habit.

Find a quiet space: Choose a quiet and peaceful environment where you can concentrate and reflect. This could be a cozy corner in your home, a park, or anywhere that helps you feel relaxed and focused.

Start with a prompt: If you're unsure about what to write, begin with a prompt or question to guide your thoughts. It could be something as simple as "How do I feel today?" or "What am I grateful for?".

Write freely: Let your thoughts flow without judgment or censorship. This isn't an essay or for someone else. Write whatever comes to mind, even if it feels messy or disorganized. Don't worry about grammar or spelling mistakes—this is your private space for self-expression.

Explore different journaling techniques: There are various journaling techniques you can try to enhance your experience. Some examples include stream-of-consciousness writing, gratitude journaling, bullet journaling, or reflective prompts.

Reflect and review: Periodically review your past entries to see patterns, insights, or progress. This can provide valuable self-awareness and a sense of personal growth.

Experiment with other forms of expression: Journaling doesn't have to be limited to writing. You can include drawings, sketches, photographs, audio/video recordings, or even collage to capture your experiences visually. What matters is being able to communicate what's inside of you in a tangible way.

Be consistent but flexible: While regular journaling is beneficial, don't feel pressured to write every single day. Be flexible with your routine and adjust it to fit your schedule and needs. If you get out of the habit, accept that and just start journaling again.

Maintain privacy: Keep your journal in a safe place where it won't be easily accessed by others. This will help you maintain the privacy and intimacy of your thoughts.

Remember, journaling is a personal practice, so feel free to adapt these suggestions to suit your own preferences and style. Enjoy the process and allow yourself to explore and discover new insights through your journaling journey.

Each week you will have a new prompt to reflect on. After reading the prompt, think about what it looks like in your life. Are there things you do well, not so well, or, perhaps, have never considered before? Write those down. After meditating on the prompt, are there any goals you'd like to make? Write those down. You will also have an assignment to carry out throughout the coming week and end with a reflective writing activity at the end of the week.

What matters is the work you do on yourself more than the words that are contained on the pages. Being willing to be honest with yourself, to really search through your thoughts and beliefs, to honestly examine what motivates you and makes you afraid, to brutally ask yourself the hard questions and then to be savagely honest with yourself, and to take risks in changing behavior and your posture towards others are really where the transformative work is found. This is the the work that can incite the changes you want in your life. Don't be afraid of yourself – you've already lived with yourself since your birth. Don't be afraid of having wrong beliefs and unfounded emotional reactions. Don't be afraid of being vulnerable. ***Lean into it.***

GROUNDING

When we embark on the journey of exploring difficult topics, grounding ourselves becomes of utmost importance. Grounding acts as an anchor, helping us remain rooted and connected to the present moment as we navigate challenging emotions and thoughts. It provides stability, safety, and a sense of balance amidst the sometimes turbulent waters of deep self-exploration. By grounding ourselves, we create a firm foundation from which we can courageously explore difficult topics, ensuring that we do so from a place of centeredness and clarity.

Grounding also allows us to cultivate resilience and maintain our well-being when confronting challenging subjects. It enables us to stay attuned to our bodies, minds, and emotions, providing a sense of stability and control amidst the discomfort that may arise. Grounding techniques, such as deep breathing, mindfulness practices, or physical activities, help us regulate our nervous system, reduce anxiety, and enhance our ability to process and integrate difficult experiences. By prioritizing grounding as we navigate challenging topics, we empower ourselves to approach them with greater self-awareness, self-compassion, and the capacity to grow and heal. It, like journaling and many aspects covered in this journal, is a discipline that we all can develop and grow.

A GROUNDING ACTIVITY

There's a multitude of grounding practices out there. The following one is a simple example that exemplifies the intent of these type of activities. Go ahead, find a comfortable spot, and give the following example an honest and sincere attempt.

Step 1: Press your feet into the ground

- Sit in a comfortable position, close your eyes, splay your toes, and press down into the floor, with equal pressure from your big toe to your small toe, from the front of your foot to the back of your heel. Feel how your foot connects to the ground and how the ground exerts a constant pressure back toward your foot.

Step 2: Concentrate on your breath

- Slowly inhale through your nose for three seconds. Try to inhale in an even controlled manner. Feel the air enter your nose, and try to identify when your inhalation begins and when it ends. Imagine the air coming into your lungs.

- Next, exhale in a controlled manner for three seconds through your mouth. Feel your breath leave your lungs and pass through your lips. Take note of when your exhalation begins and ends.

Step 3: Journal

- As practice for the next 10 weeks, take a moment and reflect on what you just experienced. Describe it on the next page. Repeat the exercise if it helps. Did you feel less or more in control? What do you think are possible reasons for that, even if you didn't feel any different? What did you think or stop thinking? Where could you use this exercise or something like it in your daily life?

WEEK 1: PRACTICING GRATITUDE

Date:

*"Gratitude is the ability to experience life as a gift.
It liberates us from the prison of self–preoccupation."*
– John Ortberg

one

Gratitude is an essential virtue that holds the power to transform our lives and the world around us. It is the genuine appreciation for the blessings, experiences, and people we encounter every day. Practicing gratitude helps us change our focus from what we don't have to what we do have, fostering a sense of contentment and fulfillment.

Practicing gratitude is associated with numerous health benefits including improved mental well-being, reduced stress levels, better sleep quality, and a stronger immune system. Yet, it may be difficult to practice gratitude when we are going through difficult times - a partner decides to leave, a loved one passes away, or I hate my job. In such times, gratitude is a discipline that grounds our perspective.

Gratitude strengthens our relationships, as expressing gratitude towards others fosters connection and deepens bonds. Moreover, it promotes resilience and emotional well-being, as it helps us navigate challenges with grace and perspective. Ultimately, gratitude is a transformative force that fuels kindness, spreads positivity, and brings about a greater sense of happiness and abundance in our lives.

Start of Week 1: Journal Prompt

Take a moment to reflect on the concept of gratitude and its impact on your life. Begin by listing five things or aspects of your life that you are grateful for. These can be big or small, tangible or intangible. Explore why each of these items holds significance to you and how they contribute to your overall well-being.

Start of Week 1: Journal Prompt

Next, consider the people who have positively influenced your life or supported you in various ways. Write about three individuals you are grateful for and the specific ways in which they have made a difference in your life. How have their actions, words, or presence impacted your journey?

_____

_____

_____

_____

_____

_____

_____

_____

_____

_____

_____

_____

_____

_____

_____

_____

_____

_____

_____

_____

_____

_____

_____

_____

_____

Now, shift your focus inward and reflect on personal qualities or strengths that you appreciate about yourself. Identify three aspects of yourself that you are grateful for and describe how they have played a role in your life's achievements or personal growth.

Week 1

Middle of Week 1: Journal Prompt

As you go through the week, spend 5 minutes each day practicing gratitude. Write them down. Is anything getting in the way of this for you? What is it? Come back to the journal at the end of week and write a reflection.

Week 1

Gratitude helps you to grow and
expand; gratitude brings joy and
laughter into your life and into the
lives of all those around you.

– Eileen Caddy –

End of Week 1: Journal Prompt

Take a moment to contemplate the past week of exploring and embracing gratitude in your life. Set aside some time for self-reflection and use the following prompt to delve deeper into your experiences:

- How has the practice of gratitude impacted your mindset and overall well-being throughout the week? Describe any shifts in your perspective or moments of increased awareness.

End of Week 1: Journal Prompt

- Reflect on the specific moments, people, or aspects of your life that you felt grateful for during this week. What made these experiences meaningful to you? Did any surprises or unexpected sources of gratitude arise?

End of Week 1: Journal Prompt

- How do you plan to integrate gratitude into your thoughts, actions, and relationships going forward?

_____

_____

_____

_____

_____

_____

_____

_____

_____

_____

_____

_____

_____

_____

_____

_____

_____

_____

_____

_____

_____

_____

_____

_____

_____

WEEK 2: EMBRACING DISCOMFORT

Date:

"Discomfort is the price of admission to a meaningful life."
– Susan David

two

Discomfort, despite its inherent unpleasantness, serves as a catalyst for growth, resilience, and self-improvement. It pushes us beyond our comfort zones, allowing us to explore new possibilities, confront challenges, and develop valuable skills. Discomfort motivates change. When we embrace discomfort, we open ourselves to valuable opportunities for learning and personal development. It forces us to adapt, innovate, and overcome obstacles, ultimately leading to increased self-confidence and a broader range of experiences. Discomfort serves as a powerful motivator, propelling us forward and enabling us to discover our true potential. By embracing discomfort, we embark on a transformative journey of growth and fulfillment.

When we face discomfort, the intensity will be greater, but the duration will be shorter.

When we avoid discomfort, the discomfort is forever.

Start of Week 2: Journal Prompt

Reflect on a time when you willingly embraced discomfort in order to grow and learn. What was the situation, and what motivated you to push beyond your comfort zone? How did you navigate the discomfort, and what did you discover about yourself in the process? Consider the lessons you learned from that experience and how it has influenced your ability to accept and embrace discomfort in other areas of your life.

Middle of Week 2: Journal Prompt

As you go through the week, become aware of the times you are faced with discomfort. How do you respond? What is it about those particular instances that is making it easier or more difficult for you? How do you want to respond differently the next time a similar situation happens? Come back to the journal at the end of week and write a reflection.

> Open your arms to change, but
> don't let go of your values.
>
> – Dalai Lama –

End of Week 2: Journal Prompt

After dedicating a week to contemplating the idea of discomfort, take a moment to reflect on your experiences and insights. Set aside some time for self-reflection and use the following prompt to delve deeper into your understanding:

- How have you approached and navigated discomfort during this week? Did you find any particular strategies or practices helpful in managing and embracing discomfort? Are there any areas where you would like to improve your ability to handle discomfort in the future?

End of Week 2: Journal Prompt

- Reflect on the potential lessons or growth opportunities that discomfort can offer. Have you discovered any valuable insights or personal growth as a result of embracing discomfort? How has your perspective on discomfort evolved over the course of this week?

End of Week 2: Journal Prompt

- Moving forward, what are some actions or habits you can incorporate into your life to better embrace and navigate discomfort? How can you use discomfort as a catalyst for growth and self-discovery? What steps can you take to build resilience and face discomfort with courage?

WEEK 3: ALLOWING HAPPINESS

Date:

"There is no way to happiness. Happiness is the way."
– Thich Nhat Hanh

three

The guilt of feeling happy is an intricate and conflicting emotion that arises from the complex interplay of personal experiences, societal expectations, and empathy towards others and ourselves. In a world with suffering and injustice, experiencing happiness can seem unjust or selfish, leading to a sense of guilt. The perception that one's own joy may come at the expense of others' well-being can create a profound internal struggle. It's important to recognize that happiness is not inherently wrong or immoral. Instead, it is an aspect of life that all humans want. By embracing happiness and maintaining compassion for the suffering of others, you can find a harmonious balance between personal joy and genuine concern for others.

Happiness that originates from within ourselves is a lasting form of joy. It's a state of contentment and fulfillment that arises from our inner being, independent of external circumstances. When we cultivate a positive mindset, practice gratitude, engage in self-care, and align with our values, we tap into the happiness within us. This internal happiness is resilient and sustainable, remaining unaffected by the ebb and flow of life's ups and downs. It's a gentle flame that radiates warmth and spreads joy to those around us, reminding us that true happiness is found within ourselves.

Start of Week 3: Journal Prompt

Take a moment to reflect on your current state of happiness and contentment. Explore any inner barriers or limiting beliefs that may prevent you from fully allowing yourself to be happy. What are recurring thoughts or patterns that hold you back from embracing joy? Are there any past experiences or traumas impacting your ability to experience happiness?

Start of Week 3: Journal Prompt

Next, imagine your life if you could fully embrace and allow yourself to be happy. How would it look and feel? Consider the positive impact it could have on various aspects of your life, such as relationships, career, and overall well-being. Identify two to three small actions or mindset shifts you can make to start allowing yourself to be happy on a regular basis. These could be self-care practices, gratitude exercises, or practicing healthy self-talk.

Middle of Week 3: Journal Prompt

As you go through the week, whenever the feeling arises, allow yourself to be happy. If you start to feel guilty, push back on this emotion. At the end of each day, write a reflection on how it went. Were you able to feel genuinely happy? Or, did guilt take over and cause you to discount the feeling of happiness? If so, what do you think was the reason for this particular instance?

Week 3

> "Happiness is when what you think, what you say, and what you do are in harmony."
> – Mahatma Gandhi –

End of Week 3: Journal Prompt

After dedicating a week to contemplating the concept of guilt-free happiness, take a moment to reflect on your experiences and insights. Set aside some time for self-reflection and use the following prompt to delve deeper into your understanding:

- Reflect on the concept of guilt-free happiness. What does it mean to you? Have you identified any specific beliefs or patterns that have hindered your ability to experience happiness without guilt? Describe any shifts or realizations you've had regarding this topic.

End of Week 3: Journal Prompt

- Throughout this week, what were some moments or situations that brought you happiness? Describe them in detail, including the emotions and sensations you experienced. How did you initially respond to these moments of joy?

End of Week 3: Journal Prompt

- Consider the origins of any guilt or shame that may arise when experiencing happiness. Have you uncovered any underlying reasons or sources for these feelings? How have they influenced your relationship with happiness in the past? Reflect on any limiting beliefs or societal expectations that may have contributed to this guilt.

End of Week 3: Journal Prompt

- Moving forward, what are some strategies or practices you can incorporate into your daily life to cultivate guilt-free happiness? How can you actively challenge and reframe any guilt-inducing thoughts or beliefs? What steps can you take to prioritize your own happiness and well-being without apology?

WEEK 4: HEALTHY BOUNDARIES

Date:

"Daring to set boundaries is about having the courage to love ourselves even when we risk disappointing others."
— Brené Brown

four

Healthy boundaries are vital for fostering healthy relationships and maintaining one's well-being. They serve as protective lines that define where our individual needs, values, and limits begin and end. Setting and enforcing boundaries empowers us to prioritize self-care, maintain our autonomy, and preserve our emotional and physical health. It enables effective communication, as it clarifies expectations and fosters mutual respect.

Healthy boundaries also help prevent burnout and resentment by establishing limits on our time, energy, and resources. They also protect the things we value and the health of relationships we already have. By practicing healthy boundaries, we create a supportive environment that promotes personal growth, emotional balance, and harmonious connections with others.

Journal Start of Week 4: Prompt

Reflect on a recent situation where you felt your boundaries were compromised or violated. Describe the details of the situation and your emotional response. Based on this experience, write about three specific actions you can start to establish that will help you maintain healthy boundaries now.

Middle of Week 4: Journal Prompt

As you go through the week, become aware of the times you need to establish boundaries with someone. If you're working on saying no, were you able to do so with kindness? If not, what was it about that particular instance that is making it difficult for you? If you're working on saying yes, how did you do? How did you feel after you said yes: anxious, regretful, happy?

> *Those who get angry when you set a boundary are the ones you need to set boundaries for.*
>
> *– J.S. Wolfe –*

End of Week 4: Journal Prompt

After dedicating a week to contemplating the concept of healthy boundaries, take a moment to reflect on your experiences and insights. Set aside some time for self-reflection and use the following prompt to delve deeper into your understanding:

- Throughout this week, what were some situations or interactions where you felt the need for healthier boundaries? Describe them in detail, including any emotions or discomfort that arose. How did you initially respond to these instances?

End of Week 4: Journal Prompt

- Reflect on the significance of healthy boundaries in your life. What does it mean to you to have healthy boundaries? Have you identified any areas or relationships where boundaries are particularly important? Describe any shifts or realizations you've had regarding the importance of setting and honoring boundaries.

End of Week 4: Journal Prompt

- Explore your personal boundaries. What are some non-negotiable values, needs, or limits that you have identified for yourself? Reflect on any instances where you compromised your boundaries in the past and the impact it had on your well-being. How can you reinforce and communicate your boundaries more effectively in the future?

- Moving forward, what are some actionable steps you can take to establish and maintain healthy boundaries in your life? How can you communicate your boundaries effectively and assertively to others? What self-care practices or habits can you integrate to support your boundary-setting journey?

WEEK 5: ACCEPTING CHANGE

Date:

"When we are no longer able to change a situation, we are challenged to change ourselves."
– Viktor Frankl

five

Accepting change is crucial for personal growth and adaptability in an ever-evolving world. Change brings new opportunities, challenges, and experiences that can broaden horizons and foster resilience. It allows individuals to break free from stagnant routines, explore uncharted territories, and embrace transformative possibilities.

By embracing change, one opens the door to personal development, innovation, and a deeper understanding of oneself and the world. It enables individuals to navigate uncertainties, overcome obstacles, and build the confidence needed to thrive in a dynamic and unpredictable world. Ultimately, accepting change is not only essential for individual growth but also for encouraging progress, innovation, and the overall betterment of society.

Start of Week 5: Journal Prompt

Reflect on a recent experience where you encountered a significant change in your life. Describe the emotions and thoughts that arose during this period of change. What were some of the initial challenges or resistance you faced? How did you eventually come to accept and adapt to the change? What valuable lessons did you learn from this experience, and how has it shaped your perspective on accepting change in general? Explore how your acceptance or unacceptance of change impacted your personal growth and transformation.

Week 5

Middle of Week 5: Journal Prompt

As you go throughout your week, become aware of the times you are faced with change. These might be small changes, like finding a new coffee shop or changes in your workplace, to big life changes, like a child heading off to college or health news. How do you find yourself responding to these changes?

Week 5

> "Progress is impossible without change, and those who cannot change their minds cannot change anything."
> – George Bernard Shaw –

End of Week 5: Journal Prompt

After dedicating a week to contemplating the concept of change, take a moment to reflect on your experiences and insights. Set aside some time for self-reflection and use the following prompt to delve deeper into your understanding:

- Throughout this week, what were some instances or areas in your life where you encountered change? Describe them in detail, including any emotions or reactions that arose. How did you initially respond to these moments of change?

End of Week 5: Journal Prompt

- Explore your attitude and mindset towards change. Are you generally open and adaptable to change, or do you tend to resist or fear it? Reflect on any fears or uncertainties that may arise when faced with change. How can you cultivate a more positive and resilient mindset when navigating change?

End of Week 5: Journal Prompt

- Moving forward, what are some strategies or practices you can incorporate into your life to embrace and navigate change more effectively? How can you develop a growth mindset and cultivate resilience in the face of change? What steps can you take to embrace uncertainty and view change as an opportunity for growth?

WEEK 6: ASKING FOR HELP

Date:

"Asking for help is never a sign of weakness. It's one of the bravest things you can do. And it can save your life."
– Lily Collins

The ability to ask for help is a cornerstone of personal growth and success. It is recognition of our limitations and an acknowledgment of the strengths of others. Asking for help fosters collaboration and strengthens relationships, whether in the workplace, in personal endeavors, or within communities. It demonstrates humility and a willingness to learn, allowing us to overcome challenges more effectively.

Seeking assistance can lead to innovative solutions and fresh perspectives that we may not have considered on our own. In a world that often glorifies self-sufficiency, understanding the importance of asking for help can be transformative, empowering individuals to achieve their goals more efficiently and with greater resilience. It is not a sign of weakness but rather of wisdom and strength to recognize when we need support and to seek it out.

Do you struggle to ask for help? Why do you think that is? There are many reasons we may struggle to ask for help. We are often walking through life with unrecognized shame, so we don't feel worthy of asking for help.

Start of Week 6: Journal Prompt

Explore when it has been difficult for you to ask for and accept help. What emotions or thoughts arise when you consider seeking assistance? How do you think reaching out for support could benefit or harm you? Explore any underlying fears or insecurities that might be holding you back.

Start of Week 6: Journal Prompt

Next, examine what areas in your life you could use help in now? Where could you use advice, help with a house project, or just a friend? What kind of help could you stretch yourself with by asking for?

Next, examine what areas in your life you could use help in now? Where could you use advice, help with a house project, or just a friend? What kind of help could you stretch yourself with by asking for?

Middle of Week 6: Journal Prompt

As you go through the week, become aware of the times you could ask for help, yet don't. What is it about that particular instance that is making it difficult for you? Come back to the journal at the end of week and write a reflection.

"*Ask for help not because you are weak. But because you want to remain strong.*"
– Les Brown –

End of Week 6: Journal Prompt

After dedicating a week to contemplating the concept of asking for help, take a moment to reflect on your experiences and insights. Set aside some time for self-reflection and use the following prompt to delve deeper into your understanding:

- Throughout this week, what were some instances or situations where you recognized the need for help? Describe them in detail, including any emotions or vulnerabilities that arose. How did you initially respond to these moments of needing assistance?

- Explore any fears or concerns that may arise when considering asking for help. What are some common worries or self-judgments that emerge in these moments? Reflect on the potential impact of these fears on your well-being and relationships. How can you challenge and overcome them?

End of Week 6: Journal Prompt

- Moving forward, what are some strategies or practices you can incorporate into your life to embrace asking for help more readily? How can you create a supportive network and foster a culture of mutual assistance? What steps can you take to cultivate a mindset of openness and vulnerability when seeking support?

WEEK 7: RELEASING FEAR

Date:

"Fear kills more dreams than failure ever will."
– Suzy Kassem

seven

Fear can be paralyzing, overwhelming. Yet releasing fear is crucial for our personal growth, well-being, and the pursuit of a fulfilling life. Fear holds us back from exploring new opportunities, taking risks, and embracing change. It limits our potential, hampers our creativity, and stifles our ability to connect with others authentically. When we release fear, we open ourselves up to possibilities, allowing us to step outside our comfort zones and embark on transformative journeys.

By shedding fear, we gain the freedom to express our true selves, cultivate courage, and develop a mindset of optimism and abundance. Releasing fear empowers us to live more fully, make choices aligned with our passions, and embrace the beauty of uncertainty as we embrace the inherent potential that lies within us.

Start of Week 7: Journal Prompt

Take a moment to reflect on the fears that may be holding you back in your life. What are some specific fears that you have been carrying? How have these fears impacted your choices, opportunities, and well-being?

Start of Week 7: Journal Prompt

Next, consider the reasons why releasing fear should be important to you. What benefits do you envision experiencing by letting go of these fears? How would your life be different if you were able to let fear go?

_____

_____

_____

_____

_____

_____

_____

_____

_____

_____

_____

_____

_____

_____

_____

_____

_____

_____

_____

_____

_____

_____

Middle of Week 7: Journal Prompt

As you go through the week, become aware of the times you feel fear. What is it about those particular instances that are causing fear? Come back to the journal at the end of the week and write a reflection.

Week 7

> *"Everything you want is on the other side of fear."*
> *– Jack Canfield –*

End of Week 7: Journal Prompt

After dedicating a week to contemplating the concept of fear, take a moment to reflect on your experiences and insights. Set aside some time for self-reflection and use the following prompt to delve deeper into your understanding:

- Throughout this week, what were some situations or thoughts that evoked fear within you? Describe them in detail, including any emotions or physical sensations that arose. How did you initially respond to these moments of fear?

_____

_____

_____

_____

_____

_____

_____

_____

_____

_____

_____

_____

_____

_____

_____

_____

_____

_____

_____

_____

_____

_____

_____

End of Week 7: Journal Prompt

- Reflect on the nature of fear. What does fear mean to you? Have you identified any patterns or beliefs about fear that have influenced your relationship with it? Describe any shifts or realizations you've had regarding the nature and impact of fear.

End of Week 7: Journal Prompt

- Reflect on the potential lessons and opportunities that fear presents. Have you discovered new perspectives, strengths, or possibilities as a result of confronting your fears? How have your emotions and thoughts evolved throughout this process? Are there any specific experiences that stand out to you?

End of Week 7: Journal Prompt

- Moving forward, what are some strategies or practices you can incorporate into your life to navigate fear more effectively? How can you develop courage and resilience in the face of fear? What steps can you take to challenge and overcome your fears, or to coexist with them in a way that allows you to move forward?

WEEK 8: SAVAGE FORGIVENESS

Date:

"We must develop and maintain the capacity to forgive. He who is devoid of the power to forgive is devoid of the power to love."
– Martin Luther King Jr.

eight

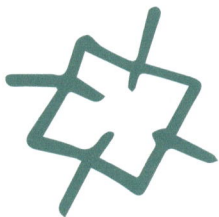

Humans are the only species on earth who have the ability to forgive one another. Think about that for a minute. Think about how important forgiveness is to have healthy relationships, healthy families, and healthy societies. Forgiving others is a profound act of compassion and personal growth. It involves releasing resentment, bitterness, and the desire for revenge, and instead choosing to let go of past hurts and grievances. Forgiveness does not mean condoning the wrong or forgetting the pain caused, but rather a conscious decision to free oneself from the emotional burden that comes with holding onto grudges. It requires empathy, understanding, and a willingness to see the humanity in others, acknowledging that everyone is capable of making mistakes, as well as changing. By forgiving others, we create space for healing, personal peace, and the possibility of restoring relationships. Ultimately, forgiveness is a powerful tool that empowers us to move forward, fostering inner harmony, and the potential for a more compassionate and harmonious world.

Start of Week 8: Journal Prompt

Reflect on a time when someone hurt or wronged you. Describe the situation, the emotions you experienced, and the struggle with forgiveness. If you forgave them, how did forgiving this person impact your own well-being and personal growth? If you didn't, how did your unforgiveness impact you? What lessons did you learn from the experience, and how has it shaped your perspective on forgiveness and compassion?

Start of Week 8: Journal Prompt

Finally, outline specific steps you can take to practice savage forgiveness in your life.

Middle of Week 8: Journal Prompt

As you go through the week, become aware of the times when someone needs forgiveness from you, when you need forgiveness from others, and when you need to forgive yourself.

Week 8

> "Without forgiveness life is governed by an endless cycle of resentment and retaliation."
> – Roberto Assagioli –

End of Week 8: Journal Prompt

After dedicating a week to contemplating the concept of forgiveness, take a moment to reflect on your experiences and insights. Set aside some time for self-reflection and use the following prompt to delve deeper into your understanding:

- Throughout this week, what were some situations, memories, or individuals that brought up the need for forgiveness? Describe them in detail, including any emotions or reactions that arose. How did you initially respond to these moments of forgiveness?

End of Week 8: Journal Prompt

- Reflect on your understanding of forgiveness. What does forgiveness mean to you? Have you identified any personal beliefs or assumptions about forgiveness that have influenced your relationship with it? Describe any shifts or realizations you've had regarding the nature and power of forgiveness.

End of Week 8: Journal Prompt

- Consider the impact of holding onto grudges or resentment. Reflect on how the act of forgiving, or the absence of forgiveness, affects your own well-being and relationships. Have you noticed any patterns or negative consequences that result from holding onto past grievances?

End of Week 8: Journal Prompt

- Moving forward, what are some strategies or practices you can incorporate into your life to cultivate forgiveness? How can you deepen your understanding of empathy, compassion, and understanding in the forgiveness process? What steps can you take to heal and let go of past hurts, both for yourself and for others?

WEEK 9: GROUNDED CONFIDENCE

Date:

"Always remember you are braver than you believe, stronger than you seem, and smarter than you think."
– Christopher Robin

nine

Grounded confidence refers to the state of being self-assured while maintaining a strong connection to reality and evidence-based reasoning. It embodies a balanced and pragmatic mindset that acknowledges both the strengths and limitations of one's knowledge and abilities. A person with grounded confidence approaches challenges and uncertainties with a healthy blend of optimism and skepticism, drawing upon their expertise and experiences while remaining open to new information and perspectives.

This mindset encourages thoughtful decision-making, fosters intellectual humility, and cultivates a willingness to learn and adapt in the face of changing circumstances. Grounded confidence serves as a foundation for personal growth, professional success, and effective collaboration with others. It also create space for healing, personal peace, and the possibility of restoring relationships.

Start of Week 9: Journal Prompt

How well do you live out grounded confidence? If you do well in this area, reflect on a situation where you exhibited grounded confidence. Describe the circumstances, the challenges you faced, and how you maintained a balanced mindset while navigating through them. How did your grounded confidence contribute to your decision-making process and overall outcome? If you do not feel you do well in this area, why do you think that is? How could grounded confidence benefit your life and those in it? How could you cultivate grounded confidence in your life?

Week 9

As you go through the week, contemplate the idea of grounded confidence. Are there circumstances where you do well? Circumstances where you don't do well?

Week 9

"*Once we believe in ourselves, we can risk curiosity, wonder, spontaneous delight, or any experience that reveals the human spirit.*"
– E. E. Cummings –

End of Week 9: Journal Prompt

After dedicating a week to contemplating the concept of grounded confidence, take a moment to reflect on your experiences and insights. Set aside some time for self-reflection and use the following prompt to delve deeper into your understanding:

- Throughout this week, what were some situations or moments where you experienced grounded confidence? Describe them in detail, including any thoughts, emotions, or actions that exemplified this sense of confidence. How did you initially respond to these moments of grounded confidence?

End of Week 9: Journal Prompt

- Reflect on your understanding of grounded confidence. What does it mean to you? Have you identified any beliefs or patterns that have influenced your relationship with confidence? Describe any shifts or realizations you've had regarding the balance between confidence and being rooted in reality.

End of Week 9: Journal Prompt

- Moving forward, what are some strategies or practices you can incorporate into your life to continue cultivating grounded confidence? How can you embrace a growth mindset and continue to build self-belief while remaining rooted in reality? What steps can you take to balance confidence with humility and openness to growth?

End of Week 9: Journal Prompt

- Moving forward, what are some strategies or practices you can incorporate into your life to continue cultivating grounded confidence? How can you embrace a growth mindset and continue to build self-belief while remaining rooted in reality? What steps can you take to balance confidence with humility and openness to growth?

WEEK 10: GROWTH MINDSET

Date:

"Live as if you were to die tomorrow; learn as if you were to live forever."
– Mahatma Gandhi

ten

Having a growth mindset is of paramount importance in personal and professional development. It is the belief that one's abilities and intelligence, one's entire person, and can be cultivated and developed through effort, perseverance, and a willingness to learn from failures and setbacks. Individuals with a growth mindset are more likely to embrace challenges, view obstacles as opportunities for growth, and persist in the face of adversity.

Someone with a growth mindset accepts the setbacks, messes, and challenges in life as opportunities for growth. They understand that talents and skills can be honed through dedication and hard work, and they are open to continuous learning and improvement. A growth mindset fosters resilience, creativity, and a passion for lifelong learning, enabling individuals to reach their full potential and achieve success in various aspects of life. People with an established growth mindset don't just wait for change but rather seek it.

Start of Week 10: Journal Prompt

Reflect on a recent challenge or setback you faced. Describe how you initially reacted to the situation and examine whether your mindset was fixed ("There's nothing I can do") or growth-oriented ("I can learn and grow from this"). What thoughts and beliefs influenced your response?

Start of Week 10: Journal Prompt

Then, consider how adopting a growth mindset could have influenced your perception of the challenge and the actions you took. How might embracing a growth mindset have led to different outcomes or opportunities for personal growth?

Start of Week 10: Journal Prompt

Finally, outline specific steps you can take to cultivate a growth mindset in future challenges and setbacks.

_____
_____
_____
_____
_____
_____
_____
_____
_____
_____
_____
_____
_____
_____
_____
_____
_____
_____
_____
_____
_____
_____
_____
_____
_____
_____

Middle of Week 10: Journal Prompt

As you go through the week, notice how you react to setbacks, mistakes, or challenges. Are you able to reframe mistakes as learning opportunities?

> *"It does not matter how slowly you go so long as you do not stop."*
> *– Confucius –*

End of Week 10: Journal Prompt

After dedicating a week to contemplating the concept of a growth mindset, take a moment to reflect on your experiences and insights. Set aside some time for self-reflection and use the following prompt to delve deeper into your understanding:

- Throughout this week, what were some situations or moments where you embraced a growth mindset? Describe them in detail, including any thoughts, emotions, or actions that exemplified this mindset. How did you initially respond to these moments of growth mindset?

End of Week 10: Journal Prompt

- Consider the benefits and challenges of a growth mindset. Reflect on how adopting a growth mindset has influenced your thoughts, behaviors, and overall perspective. Have you noticed any specific areas of growth or improvement as a result of embracing this mindset? Are there any obstacles or areas where you can further develop a growth mindset?

End of Week 10: Journal Prompt

- Reflect on the impact of embracing a growth mindset on your goals and aspirations. How has this mindset influenced your willingness to take risks, embrace learning opportunities, and pursue personal growth? Describe any experiences or instances where your growth mindset has empowered you to stretch beyond your comfort zone.

- Moving forward, what are some strategies or practices you can incorporate into your life to continue cultivating a growth mindset? How can you nurture a mindset that embraces learning, growth, and resilience? What steps can you take to challenge and overcome limiting beliefs or fixed mindset thinking?

> *"Smooth seas do not make skillful sailors."*
> *– African Proverb –*

CONCLUSION

The concept of radical acceptance offers a powerful approach to navigating life's challenges and finding inner peace. Through this practice, individuals are encouraged to embrace reality as it is, without judgment or resistance. Radical acceptance invites us to let go of the struggle against circumstances we cannot change and instead focus our energy on finding meaning, growth, and contentment within the present moment.

By cultivating radical acceptance, we can develop a greater sense of self-awareness and emotional resilience. We learn to acknowledge and honor our thoughts, feelings, and experiences without trying to control or suppress them. This nonjudgmental stance allows us to develop a healthier relationship with ourselves and others, fostering compassion, empathy, and understanding.

Furthermore, radical acceptance promotes psychological well-being by reducing stress and increasing mental flexibility. When we stop resisting what is, we free ourselves from unnecessary suffering and open up space for personal growth. By accepting reality, we become better equipped to adapt to change, overcome adversity, and make healthier choices for ourselves.

Radical acceptance is not about resignation or passivity; rather, it is an empowering practice that encourages us to take responsibility for our own happiness and well-being. It invites us to actively engage with life while surrendering our attachment to specific outcomes. By embracing the present moment, we can make conscious choices and take meaningful action, guided by our values and inner wisdom.

In a world that is constantly changing and often unpredictable, radical acceptance offers a guiding principle that can bring us closer to peace and fulfillment. It allows us to find beauty and purpose even in the midst of chaos and uncertainty. By letting go of resistance and embracing reality, we create a foundation for personal growth, authentic relationships, and a more harmonious existence.

Ultimately, radical acceptance is a lifelong journey—a practice that requires patience, self-compassion, and consistent effort. As we continue to cultivate this mindset, we develop the capacity to live fully and authentically, embracing both the joys and sorrows that life presents. By adopting radical acceptance as a guiding principle, we embark on a path of self-discovery, resilience, and profound transformation.

ABOUT THE AUTHOR

Dr. Don Schweitzer is a licensed counselor and mindfulness coach whose practice focuses on a holistic approach to overall health, emphasizing the mind-body connection. He offers individual counseling, workshops, and classes using evidence-based practices, such as cognitive-behavioral theory and mindfulness-based interventions.

Don also provides coaching services to help clients identify and achieve their goals, using a client-centered approach tailored to meet individual needs. He is a Certified Trauma Professional and incorporates mind-body practices when appropriate. He is an experienced public speaker and communicator.

Don holds a PhD in Social Work and Social Research from Portland State University, in addition to a Bachelor's degree in Social Work from Idaho State University and a Master's degree in Social Work from Boise State University. When not working, Don enjoys hiking, riding bikes, and spending time in nature. He is dedicated to making a positive impact on the world and supporting various philanthropic causes and organizations.

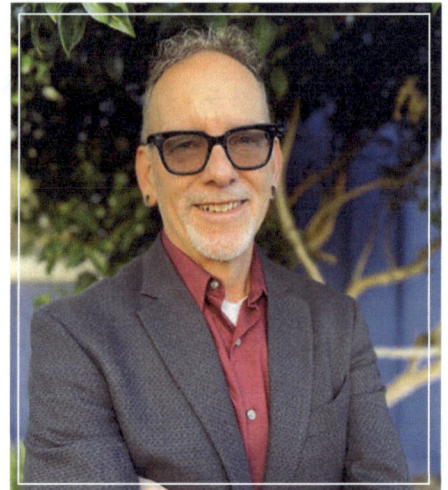

For free resources and insights, visit:
www.SierraCounselingAndCoaching.com

Made in United States
Troutdale, OR
05/12/2024